This book belongs to:

_____

This silk hat from 18th century Europe is decorated with a brightly colored bouquet of flowers. Draw the person wearing it.

Write a story about the person you just drew.

This painting shows overlapping circles in rainbow colors. Called "Ascending Suns," it was created by dyeing and hand-folding Japanese paper.

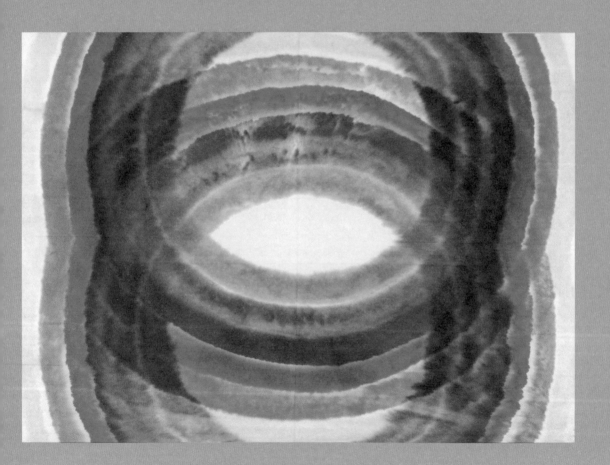

Color in these circles to create your own rainbow design.

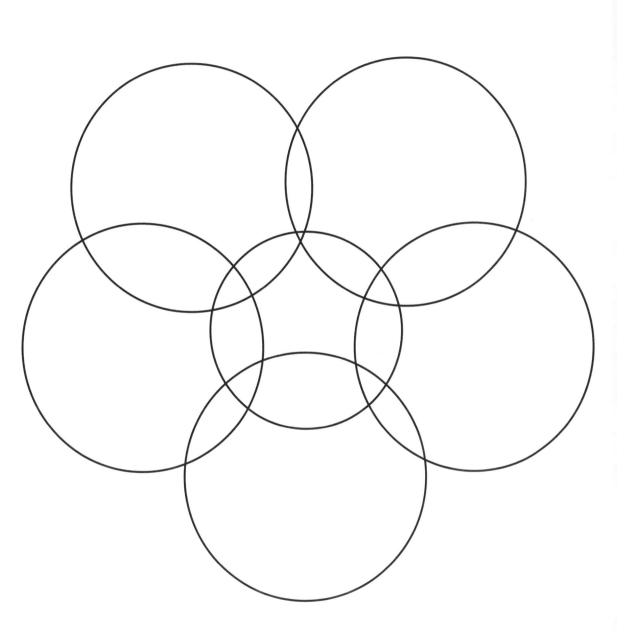

This telephone was designed by Henry Dreyfuss for the Bell Telephone Company around 1937. It became the standard phone in many homes for decades.

Draw a scene around the phone that tells a story.

These two patterns are made of flowers, but they look very different.

Draw your own pattern using your favorite flowers.

This brooch looks like a basket filled with flowers. It may have originally been a part of a tiara or a hair ornament. It was made of diamonds, silver, and gold, sometime between 1750 and 1800.

Design your own brooch to complete this woman's hairstyle.

Plates can be practical or very decorative. These are from very different time periods.

1938

1686-1701

1950s

1870s

Design 4 plates in different styles.

This iron and bronze Art Deco gate was designed by Rene Chambellan in 1928. It was installed inside a building in New York City. What do you imagine is behind this gate? Draw your design.

This toothbrush was designed by James O'Halloran in 1983. It was easy to hold and came in right and left-handed models. Design your own toothbrush.

The composition of these drawings is the same but they use different color combinations.

Chairs can be different shapes and sizes. These are all different colors and were made in different decades.

1965

1944

1936

1937-1947

Design your own chair. Is it hard or soft? What color is it?

This Chinese vase was made from glazed porcelain sometime in the 17th or 18th century. Add an arrangement of flowers to the vase.

Write a poem inspired by this vase.

This double staircase model was designed by "R.B." in France. Apprentices would create these models to learn the basic concepts of staircase design.

Design a house or a room around this whimsical staircase.

Ladies used to carry fans as part of their outfits. These fans were made in the 18th century from materials like linen, paper, and ivory.

Design your own fan. Think about what materials you will use.

These are examples of what some radios looked like in the 1950s.

What do you think radios will look like in 25 years? Draw your radio here.

Louis Comfort Tiffany was famous for his beautiful lamps. This one, called "Dragonfly" light, has dragonflies on the shade, and a gold base that looks like lilypads. It was designed between 1900 and 1910.

Design a different shade for this lamp.

This hand-painted scene from China uses many different colors. Add birds and flowers to the tree in the scene next to it and color it in.

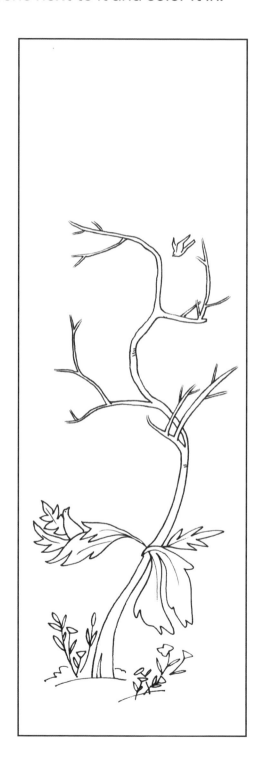

This light bulb is made of two looped and angled glass tubes. It was designed by Samuel Wilkinson in 2010. Design your own light bulb of the future.

Thomas Heatherwick's "Spun" chair looks like a very big spinning top. It is comfortable to sit in no matter which way it leans.

Can you think of another toy that could be a piece of furniture if it was very large? Draw it here.

The pattern on this Japanese kimono was made by using a stencil to print on the fabric.

Create your own pattern on this kimono.

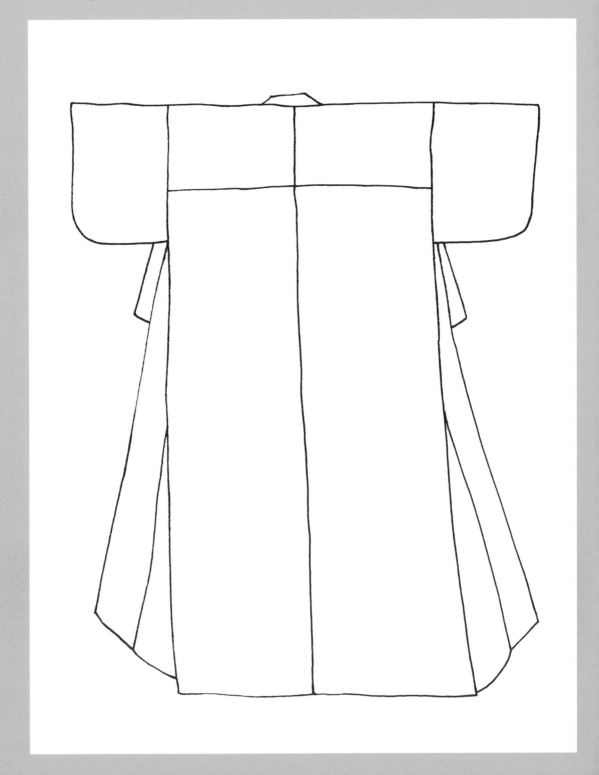

This woodcut of Mannen Bridge in Japan was made in 1830. You can see Mt. Fuji in the distance.

Design your own bridge below, then write a poem describing the scene around the bridge.

This plate was made in the Netherlands in the early 1700s. It is glazed in blue and white.

What colors would you use for your version of this plate?

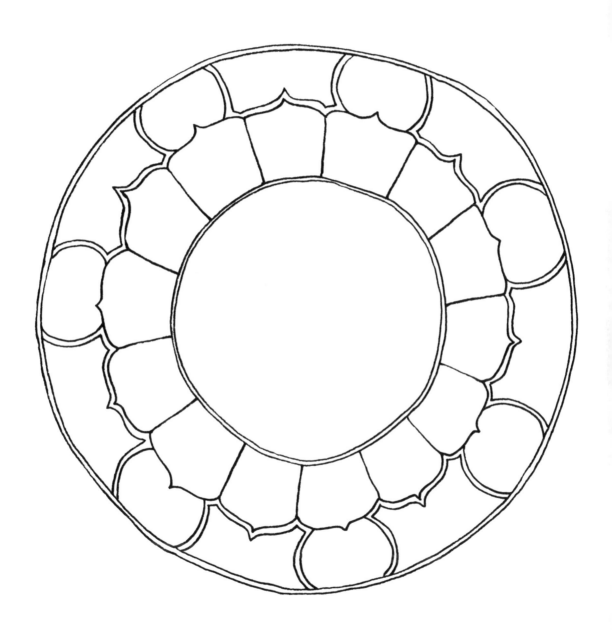

This glass vase is called the "Peacock" vase because the shape looks like a peacock tail. Add flowers to the vase.

Design your own vase inspired by an animal.

This is a portrait miniature. It is just over 3 inches high. People carried or wore these before they had photographs. A lock of hair was often included on the back. This one also included a box.

Draw portrait miniatures of people you care about.

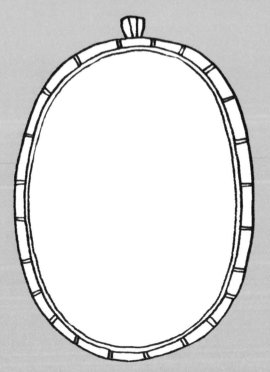

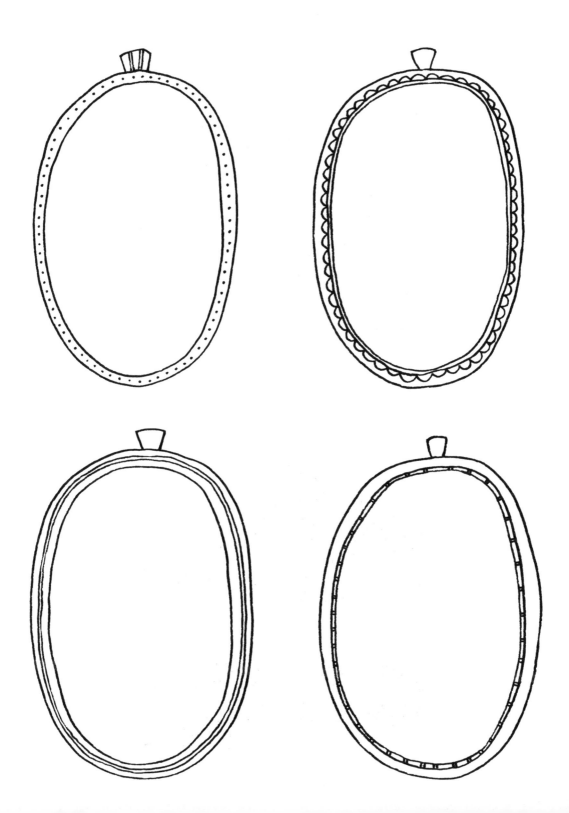

Here are two different sneakers designed by Nike. The colors are very bright and eye-catching.

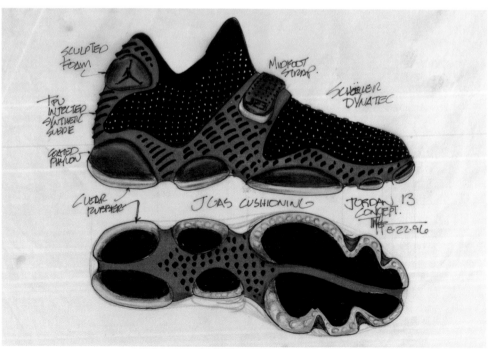

Design your own pair of sneakers.

Elenhank Designers, Inc. created "Kids and Kites" in 1964. The kites in this fabric design are all different colors, shapes, and sizes.

Choose your own colors for the kites below.

Sometimes lights can look funky, like this "PH Artichoke" light designed in Denmark in 1958.

Design your own light fixture. Is it inspired by a fruit, vegetable, or flower?

These large, colorful birds were drawn for a magazine cover in 1939.

Draw your own birds on these branches.

Michael Eden created this urn using 3D printing. He designed a complex surface that would be impossible to create using traditional ceramics.

Draw a scene around the urn using only bright colors.

Frank Gehry, a famous architect, designed this chaise lounge in 1988. It is made of cardboard— an unusual material for a chair. His side chair and lounge chair were also designed using cardboard.

Design your own chairs using odd materials. Are your chairs for lounging or sitting up straight?

This Russian teapot was made from porcelain during the late 19th to early 20th century. Draw a scene around it. How many teacups are there? What does the tablecloth look like?

A Chinese rank badge is a piece of tapestry that tells you the status of the official wearing it. This one was made before 1644. A badge with cranes indicated the highest possible rank for a scholar.

What image would you use to indicate the most important person?
Create your own rank badges to decorate this jacket.

Clocks can come in many shapes and sizes. Here are examples of what some clocks looked like in the 1930s and 1940s.

1931

1930

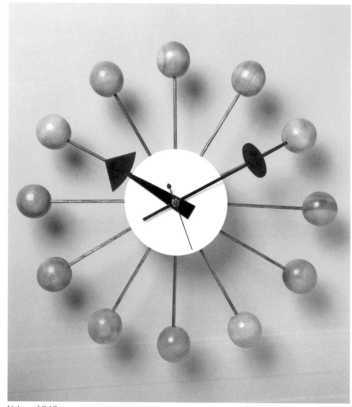

Nelson, 1949

Design your own clock here.

Sample, *Ribbons*, 1957. Alexander Hayden Girard (American, 1907–1993). Screen-printed silk. 60 x 60 cm (23 ½ in). Gift of Alexander H. Girard. 1969-165-65. Photo: Matt Flynn © Smithsonian Institution. Reproduced by permission of the designer © 1957 Girard Studio, LLC. All rights reserved.

Man's Hat, France or Italy, 18th century. Silk brocaded with metallic yarns and metal strips. 27 x 60 cm (10 5/8 x 23 5/8 in). Gift of Richard C. Greenleaf in memory of his mother, Adeline E. Greenleaf. 1952-47-2. Photo: Matt Flynn © Smithsonian Institution.

Sidewall, *Ascending Suns*, 1958–1970. Barbara White (American). Hand-folded and dyed Japanese paper. 66 x 93 cm (26 x 36 5/8 in). Gift of Barbara White. 2000-64-41. Photo: Matt Flynn © Smithsonian Institution. Reproduced by permission of the designer © Barbara White.

Telephone, *Model 302*, ca. 1937. Designed by Henry Dreyfuss (American, 1904–1972). Manufactured by Western Electric Manufacturing Company, made for Bell Telephone Company (United States). Metal, paper, rubber-sheathed cord. 14 x 23 x 18.5 cm (5 ½ x 9 1/16 x 7 5/16 in). Museum purchase from the Decorative Arts Association Acquisition Fund. 1994-73-2. Photo: Hiro Ihara © Smithsonian Institution.

Drawing, *Juniblumen: Steel Blue Background*, 1923–1932. Felice Rix-Ueno (Austrian, 1893–1967). Brush and gouache on paper. Museum purchase from Smithsonian Collections Acquisition and Decorative Arts Association Acquisition Funds. 1988-62-809. Photo: Matt Flynn © Smithsonian Institution.

Textile, England, 1810–1815. Block-printed cotton. 96 x 63.5 cm (37 13/16 x 25 in). Gift of Cora Ginsburg. 1987-70-1. Photo: Matt Flynn © Smithsonian Institution.

Brooch, England or France, 1750–1800. Diamonds (rose-cut), silver, gold. 5.1 x 7.4 x 1.2 cm (2 x 2 15/16 x ½ in). 1962-26-1. Gift of Gertrude Sampson. Photo: Dennis Cowley © Smithsonian Institution.

Plate, *Travel*, ca. 1938. Eric Ravilious (English, 1903–1942). Manufactured by Wedgwood (England). Glazed earthenware. 2 x 25.3 cm (13/16 x 9 15/16 in). Gift of Paul Walter. 1992-42-3. Photo: Dennis Cowley © Smithsonian Institution.

Dish, 1686–1701. Attributed to Adiaen Kocx (Greek, d. 1701) for the Greek A Factory (Netherlands). Tin-glazed earthenware. 3 x 34.5 x 34.5 cm (1 3/16 x 13 9/16 x 13 9/16 in). Bequest of Walter Phelps Warren. 1986-61-42. Photo: Dennis Crowley © Smithsonian Institution.

Dinner Plate, 1950s. Gabriel Pasadena (American). Glazed earthenware. 2 x 25 cm (13/16 x 9 13/16 in). Gift of Mel Byars, The Mel Byars Collection of 20th Century Design. 1990-15-9. Photo: Dennis Cowley © Smithsonian Institution.

Plate, France, ca. 1870. Joseph-Théodore Deck (1823–1891). Glazed earthenware. 6.5 x 42 cm (2 9/16 x 16 9/16 in). Gift of Eleanor Garnier Hewitt. 1931-40-37. Photo: Unknown © Smithsonian Institution.

Gate, 1928. René Paul Chambellan (American, 1893–1955). Wrought iron, bronze. 189.2 x 114.3 x 11.4 cm (74 ½ x 45 x 4 ½ in). Gift of Marcy Chanin. 1993-135-2. Photo: Dennis Cowley © Smithsonian Institution.

Toothbrush, The "*Radius*," 1983. James O'Halloran. Manufactured by Radius (United States). Celulose, nylon. 6.5 x 4 x 2.5 cm (2 9/16 x 1 9/16 x 1 in). Gift of David McFadden. 1991-91-25. Photo: Hiro Ihara © Smithsonian Institution.

Drawing, *Purpurnelke (Purple Carnation): Red with Teal and Brown*, designed 1924. Felice Rix-Ueno (Austrian, 1893–1967) for Wiener Werkstätte (Austria). Brush and gouache, graphite on paper. 35.1 x 29.8 cm (13 13/16 x 11 ¾ in). Museum purchase from Smithsonian Collections Acquisition and Decorative Arts Association Acquisition Funds. 1988-62-893. Photo: Matt Flynn © Smithsonian Institution.

Drawing, *Purpurnelke: Pale Blue with Grape and Coral*. Felice Rix-Ueno (Austrian, 1893–1967) for Wiener Werkstätte (Austria). Brush and gouache on paper. 35.1 x 29.8 cm (13 13/16 x 11 ¾ in). Museum purchase from Smithsonian Collections Acquisition and Decorative Arts Association Acquisition Funds. 1988-62-891. Photo: Matt Flynn © Smithsonian Institution.

Chair, 1965. Warren Platner (American, 1919–2006) for Knoll Associates, Inc. (United States). Bronze-plated steel, nylon upholstery. 73.5 x 68 x 54 cm (28 15/16 x 26 ¾ x 21 ¼ in). Gift of Knoll Associates, Inc. 1971-16-1. Photo: John White © Smithsonian Institution.

Child's Chair, 1944. Charles Eames (American, 1907–1978) and Ray Eames (American, 1912–1988), manufactured by Evans Products Company and distributed by Herman Miller Furniture Company (United States). Molded laminated plywood, red stain. 36.5 x 32.5 x 29 cm (14 3/8 x 12 13/16 x 11 7/16 in). Gift of Mrs. Eric Larrabee. 1991-144-1. Photo: Steve Tague © Smithsonian Institution.

Long Chair, 1936. Designed by Marcel Breuer (American, b. Hungary, 1902–1981). Manufactured by Isokon Furniture Company (England). Bent birch (frame), bent and molded birch-faced plywood (seat). 74 x 62.6 x 136 cm (29 1/8 x 24 5/8 x 53 9/16 in). Museum purchase through gift of George R. Kravis II, Anonymous Donor, and Judy Francis Zankel. 2013-17-1. Photo: Matt Flynn © Smithsonian Institution.

Chair, ca. 1947. Louis Dierra. Manufactured by Pittsburgh Plate Glass Company. Plate glass, metal, textile. 36.5 x 32.5 x 29 cm (14 3/8 x 12 13/16 x 11 7/16 in). Museum purchase through gift of George R. Kravis II and from General Acquisitions Endowment Fund. 2013-1-1. Photo: Ellen McDermott © Smithsonian Institution.

Vase, China, 17th–18th century. Glazed porcelain. 43 x 17.5 cm (16 15/16 x 6 7/8 in). Gift from the Collection of Stanley Siegel. 1976-83-1. Photo: Unknown © Smithsonian Institution.

Stairway model, France, 1850–1900. Made by "R.B." Cherry. 48.6 x 33.5 cm (19 1/8 x 13 3/16 in). Gift of Eugene V. and Clare E. Thaw. 2007-45-9. Photo: James Hart © Smithsonian Institution.

Fan, France, ca. 1750. Painted silk leaf, embroidered with metallic yarns and sequins; carved, incised, and pierced ivory sticks with applied metallic foil. 26 x 47 cm (10 ¼ x 18 ½ in). Bequest of Sarah Cooper Hewitt. 1931-6-117. Photo: Matt Flynn © Smithsonian Institution.

Fan, England, 1780–1790. Cut and painted paper leaf, ivory sticks with applied metallic foil. 26.7 x 46 cm (10 ½ x 18 1/8 in). Gift of Mrs. Robertson D. Ward, from the collection of her mother, Mrs. Helen Wright-Clark Dawson. 1970-58-25. Photo: Matt Flynn © Smithsonian Institution.

Radio, Model D25WE, 1952. Manufactured by Crosley Radio Corporation (United States). Plastic, metal. 19.2 x 33.8 x 19 cm (7 9/16 x 13 5/16 x 7 ½ in). Gift of Barbara and Max Pine. 1993-133-33. Photo: Unknown © Smithsonian Institution.

Radio, Model 11-115U or Serenader, 1951. Manufactured by Crosley Radio Corporation (United States). Plastic, metal. 14.2 x 22 x 16 cm (5 9/16 x 8 11/16 x 6 5/16 in). Gift of Barbara and Max Pine. 1993-133-35. Photo: Ellen McDermott © Smithsonian Institution.

Radio, SK 25, 1955. Designed by Fritz Eichler (American, b. 1911) and Artur Bruan (American, b. 1925). Manufactured by Braun AG (United States). Plastic, metal. 15 x 23.5 x 13.5 cm (5 7/8 x 9 ¼ x 5 5/16 in). Gift of Barry Friedman and Patricia Pastor. 1986-99-16. Photo: Dave King © Smithsonian Institution.

Lamp shade and base, Dragonfly and Lilypad, 1900–10. Designed by Clara Driscoll (American, 1861–1933) and Louis Comfort Tiffany (American, 1848-1933). Produced by Tiffany Studios (United States). Glass, lead, brass, bronze, gilding. 54.5 x 53 cm (21 7/16 x 20 7/8 in). Gift of Mrs. Margaret Carnegie Miller. 1977-111-1-a/c. Photo: Dennis Cowley © Smithsonian Institution.

Scenic, China, 1800–1830. Hand painted on joined sheets of handmade paper. 342.9 x 111.8 cm (11ft 3 in x 44 in). Museum purchase from General Acquisitions Endowment Fund. 2013-10-1. Photo: Matt Flynn © Smithsonian Institution.

Light Bulb, Plumen 001, 2010. Designed by Samuel Wilkinson (English, b. 1977) for Hulger Design Ltd (England). Glass, ABS plastic, wire, electronics. Gift of Hulger. 2011-39-1. Photo: Ellen McDermott © Smithsonian Institution.

Chair, Spun, 2010. Designed by Thomas Heatherwick (English, b. 1970). Manufactured by Magis S.p.A (Italy). Produced by Herman Miller Furniture Company (United States). Polyethylene. 66 x 91.4 cm (26 x 36 in). Gift of Herman Miller, Inc. 2012-18-1. Photo: Ellen McDermott © Smithsonian Institution.

Kimono, Japan, 1925–1945. Silk, stencil-printed in warp and weft (meisen). 147.3 x 123.2 cm (28 x 48 ½ in). Museum purchase from Friends of Textiles and General Acquisitions Endowment Funds. 2013-15-1. Photo: Matt Flynn © Smithsonian Insitution.

Print, Under Mannen Bridge at Fukagawa, from Thirty-Six Views of Fuji, ca. 1830. Woodcut on paper. 35.5 x 45.9 cm (14 x 18 1/16 in). Gift of the Estate of Mrs. Robert H. Patterson. 1941-31-115. Photo: Matt Flynn © Smithsonian Institution.

Plate, 1691–1721. Manufactured by Lambertus Van Eenhoorn and the Metal Pot Factory (Netherlands). Tin glazed earthenware. 3.5 x 26.5 cm (1 3/8 x 10 7/16 in). Bequest of Walter Phelps Warren. 1986-61-47. Photo: Unknown © Smithsonian Institution.

Vase, Peacock, ca. 1901. Louis Comfort Tiffany (American, 1848–1933), produced by Tiffany Studios (United States). Blown glass. 33.7 x 25 x 14 cm (13 ¼ x 9 13/16 x 5 ½ in). Gift of Stanley Siegel, from the Stanley Siegel Collection. 1975-32-11. Photo: Dave King © Smithsonian Institution.

Portrait Miniature, England or United States, 1780–1800. Gold, glass, hair. 8 x 5.8 x 1 cm (3 1/8 x 2 5/16 x 3/8 in). Bequest of Sarah Cooper Hewitt. 1931-6-45. Photo: Unknown © Smithsonian Institution.

Shoes, Flyknit Racer, 2009–2012. Designed by Ben Shaffer (American). Manufactured by Nike, Inc. (United States). Knitted polyester, Kevlar. 10.4 x 10.5 x 29 cm (4 1/8 x 4 1/8 x 11 7/16 in). Gift of Nike, Inc. 2012-4-1-a.b. Photo: Matt Flynn © Smithsonian Institution.

Drawing, Concept Design for Air Jordan XIII Sneaker, 1996. Designed by Tinker Hatfield (American, b. 1952). Manufactured by Nike, Inc. (United States). Black and color marking pens, turquoise and blue crayon on tracing paper. 44.8 x 60.3 x 2.5 cm (17 5/8 x 23 ¾ x 1 in). Gift of Nike. 2002-1-1. Photo: Matt Flynn © Smithsonian Institution. Reproduced by permission of the designer © Nike, Inc. 1996.

Textile, Kids and Kites, 1964. Elenhank Designers Inc. (United States). Printed cotton, linen. 250 x 147 cm (8 ft 2 7/16 in x 57 7/8 in). Gift of Henry C. and Eleanor Kluck. 1985-84-8. Photo: Matt Flynn © Smithsonian Institution. Reproduced by permission of the Estate of Henry C. and Eleanor Kluck © Elenhank Designers Inc.

Hanging Lamp, *PH Artichoke*, 1958. Designed by Poul Henningsen (Danish, 1894-1967. Manufactured by Louis Poulson & Co. (Denmark). Copper, steel, enameled metal. 69 x 84 cm (27 3/16 x 33 1/16 in). Museum purchase from General Exhibition Funds. 1983-16-1. Photo: Dave King © Smithsonian Institution.

Drawing, *Proposed Cover for "The New Yorker Magazine" or "Promenade Magazine,"* ca. 1939. Christina Malman (American, 1912-1959). Graphite, pen and ink, brush and watercolor, crayon on off-white laid paper. 48.8 x 39.3 cm (19 3/16 x 15 ½ in). Gift of Christina Malman. 1947-110-3. Photo: John Parnell © Smithsonian Institution.

Urn, *Tall Green Bloom*, 2012. Michael Eden (British, b. 1955). 3-D printed Nylon. 41 x 18 cm (16 1/8 x 7 1/16 in). Museum purchase through gift of Elizabeth and Lee Ainslie and General Acquisitions Endowment Fund. 7622-1-2013. Photo: Ellen McDermott © Smithsonian Institution.

Chaise Longue, *Bubbles*, ca. 1988. Designed by Frank O. Gehry (Canadian, b. 1929). Manufactured by New City Editions (United States). Cardboard. 87.6 x 219.1 x 73.7 cm (34 ½ x 7 ft 2 ¼ in x 29 in). Museum purchase from the Members' Acquisitions Fund of Cooper Hewitt, National Design Museum. 2012-3-1. Photo: Ellen McDermott © Smithsonian Institution.

Side Chair, ca. 1970. Frank O. Gehry (Canadian, b. 1929). Corrugated cardboard, masonite. 82.5 x 42 x 51 cm (32 ½ x 16 9/16 x 20 1/16 in). Gift of William Woolfenden. 1988-79-1. Photo: Ellen McDermott © Smithsonian Institution.

Lounge Chair, *Easy Edges*, ca. 1971. Frank O. Gehry (Canadian, b. 1929). Corrugated cardboard, masonite. 76 x 59.5 x 99 cm (29 15/16 x 23 7/16 x 39 in). Gift of William Woolfenden. 1988-79-2. Photo: John White © Smithsonian Institution.

Teapot and Lid, late 19th–early 20th century. Manufactured by Gardner Porcelain Factory (Russia). Enameled and gilt porcelain. 17.3 x 22 cm (6 13/16 x 8 11/16 in). Gift of Anna Kayaloff. 1990-117-1-a,b. Photo: Ellen McDermott © Smithsonian Institution.

Rank badge (buzi), China, 1368-1644. Silk and metallic tapestry (k'ossu) . 34 x 31.1 cm (13 3/8 x 12 ¼ in). Gift of John Pierpont Morgan. 1902-1-433. Photo: Scott Hyde © Smithsonian Institution.

Wall Clock, *I-25 clock* or *Atomic clock*, ca. 1949. Designed by George Nelson (American, 1907–1986). Manufactured by Howard Miller Clock Company (United States). Wood, painted wood, steel, sheet metal. 33.3 x 6.5 cm (13 1/8 x 2 9/16 in). Gift of The Mel Byars Collection. 1991-26-1. Photo: Matt Flynn © Smithsonian Institution.

Clock, *Big Ben*, 1931. Designed by Henry Dreyfuss (American, 1904–1972). Manufactured by Westclox (United States). Metal, glass, paper. 13.5 x 12.6 x 6.1 cm (5 5/16 x 4 15/16 x 2 3/8 in). Museum purchase through gift of Neil Sellin. 1999-2-1. Photo: Ellen McDermott © Smithsonian Institution.

Clock, *304* or *Zephyr*, ca. 1930. Designed by Kem Weber (American, 1889–1963). Manufactured by Lawson Time, Inc. (United States). Copper, brass, plastic. 9.2 x 20.6 x 8.3 cm (3 5/8 x 8 1/8 x 3 ¼ in). Museum purchase from the Decorative Arts Association Acquisition Fund. 1994-73-3. Photo: Dave King © Smithsonian Institution.

Smithsonian Design Museum

28 West 44th Street, New York, NY 10036
161-165 Farringdon Road, London, EC1R 3AL

Designed in the U.S.A.
Printed in Dongguan, China

Illustrations © Abigail Halpin
Design © Mudpuppy
www.mudpuppy.com
05/2014 M012214A

Printed with nontoxic inks.

mudpuppy

ISBN: 978-0-7353-4188-3
9 780735 341883